When God Allows Pain to Be A Factor

ISBN: 978-1-7350143-7-1

LOC Control #: 2020910957

Copyright © Terra DeVon

Publisher and Editor: Fiery Beacon Publishing House

Fiery Beacon Consulting and Publishing Group

Photography: Miles Darden

Graphics: Fiery Beacon Graphics

Blu'Cherry Photography

This work was produced in Greensboro, North Carolina, United States of America.

When God Allows Pain to be a Factor

By Terra DeVon

TABLE OF CONTENTS

The Dedication
The Introduction

My Life...

"He heals the brokenhearted and binds up their wounds."

Psalm 147:3

To every person who played a part in helping to create and cultivate my story.....

To every person that has encouraged me through this process of manifested victory....

This book is for you.

The Introduction

Pain has a way of causing people to grow. It seems strange however, it is a fact. Many of us would still be stagnant if not for the pain God allowed us to go through. It does not seem fair that God would allow the ones He loves to feel the evil sting of pain, but if God had not allowed us to endure painful situations many of us would still be going around the same mountain. God had to allow pain to be your best friend for a season or even seasons because pain did what most friends will not do, and that is, push you. Pain will push you into your destiny, pain will push you into your purpose, but even greater than this, pain will push you closer to God. It was during my painful seasons that I grew in my relationship with God. There are times when God will allow us to hurt so that it will put us in a position to cry out for His help. When God allows us to face painful seasons it is not to harm us but instead, is sent to shift us into right standing with Him.

"Before I formed you in the womb, I knew you, before you were born, I set you apart: I appointed you as a prophet to the nations."

Jeremiah 1:5(NIV)

There are those of us that had Jesus' blood stain seal upon us before we really understood why Jesus died on the cross (this is why it seemed like for many of us everything that we tried to do that was against the nature of God fought against us.) Many of us tried to be in the in crowd but sooner or later the in crowd rejected us. There is no pain like the sting of rejection; I would rather be stung by one hundred bees than to have to feel the evil sting of rejection. Unfortunately, I know what being rejected feels like all too well seeing that I endured being rejected by my own parents. I did not understand how dysfunctional I was until I developed a real relationship with Christ. It took the pain of not feeling genuine love from the two people that were supposed to have loved me unconditionally to understand the love of God.

God loved me beyond my faults and no matter what I had done He was not going to let me go. However, in feeling God's love, He still allowed pain to visit me. The pain that God allows is always to help us. Pain does a tilling within us. This spiritual tilling is needed to break up the crusted parts within us which allows God to do the necessary planting. During the spiritual tilling, God goes into the depths of our inner being and snatches out the weeds that have been planted throughout our life.

Pain is a major factor when it comes to tilling. Pain is never welcomed, but if we really understood the importance of pain we would rejoice. Pain is an indicator that many times for a believer they are on the right track. The word of God says in 1 Peter 4:12-13(ESV):

"Beloved, do not be surprised at the fiery trial when it

comes upon you to test you, as though something strange were happening to you. But rejoice insofar as you share Christ's sufferings, that you may also rejoice and be glad when his glory is revealed.

My God! God's glory is revealed through our pain, and it is because of this we should embrace our painful seasons. I did not say make pain our master and then sulk in pity parties; what I am saying is, we should embrace our painful seasons because our pain produces God's glory. Some people may not understand the purpose of this book, but God has breathed on me in this hour to encourage His people that are going through or have gone through a painful season and are still feeling the effects of pain. When God allows one of His own to feel the blunt force of pain we are guaranteed if we do not buck, because bucking delays the process. We are guaranteed to come out of the process a victor. Allow me to have a quick sidebar. There are a lot of individuals who claim to be anointed but whine every time they are faced with a trial. We cannot

profess to be anointed and shun pain at the same time. There

must be pain for the anointing to be produced. The anointing

comes with a pressing. The purpose for the pressing is to

squeeze the oil God has placed within us, out. At times it can

feel like your very life is being squeezed out, however this

process is mandatory to do what God has called you to. You

cannot operate in the anointing effectively if you are not willing

to go through painful seasons. You will only continue to be a

squeaky wheel.

I want to go back to a comment I mentioned earlier; I

think it is imperative that I expound on what I meant about

embracing pain. When we make the choice to embrace our

painful seasons, that is saying that we trust God with what He

is wanting to develop out of the process. When we put our trust

in God during this time it will take our focus off the pain and

shift our focus on God. Isaiah 26:3(ESV) reminds us,

"You keep him in perfect peace whose mind is stayed on you, because he trusts in you."

When we keep our focus on God it causes us to feel the peace of God. So yes, you will go through the pain, but you will go through it knowing you have God's peace. Many in the body are succumbing to their pain because their focus is off. Our seasons of pain requires us to lean on God; this also helps usher in God's peace. Even while going through dark nights, God's peace will be evident.

Chapter 1

My Life, My Pain

I am a product of adultery. My mother was married when she got pregnant by my dad. It was shared with me that my mom and dad were high school lovers. They continued to see one another after my mom got married which produced yours truly. I was told that my mom's husband took one look at me and immediately knew that I was not his child. It was stated that he left me and my mom at the hospital. Oh yes, I am the splitting image of my dad, which makes it even harder to believe that I have had to endure so much pain through him. Before I delve into that part of my life allow me to give you a little history of when I was an infant. My mom was raised by an aunt who was her mom's sister.

Let's have a side bar. My grandmother gave my mom to her sister to raise, my mom gave me to her mom to raise and my daughter was taken from me due to no fault of my own. It was very sinister how my daughter was taken but we will get into that later in the book - I just wanted to show you the cycle in my family. My grandmother was not raised by her mom. My grandmother's mom died when my grandmother was very young and was raised by different siblings, I was told. This was a cycle conjured up by the enemy, I believe. The aunt that raised my mom did not like my dad, and because of her dislike for him, and because I was not my mom's husband's child, she would not babysit for my mom when she wanted to go out, so this caused my mom to have to take me with her. It was shared with me that when she wanted to go to the club, she would take me and leave me asleep in the car. I was told that I was unkempt and in danger.

My grandmother and some other family members had come from Charlotte to Alabama for a funeral. While my grandmother was there her sister "the aunt" that raised my mom told her that if she did not want to have to come back to another funeral, she would need to take me with her. After my mom and grandmother talked, my mom came in and placed me on my grandmother's lap, and said, "if I'm not there to get her in six months you can have her." My grandmother was the only real mother that I have known, but something was still missing.

Now, before I share what I believe was missing allow me to address a few things. In no way am I trying to belittle my mom, I love her. The only thing I hate is that I never had a real relationship with her however, the fact remains the same I will not belittle her through my writing. I did go back in my teenage years to live with my mom for a short period of time. During the time that I lived with her there was still no genuine relationship between my mom and I. To her defense I will say this: it is hard to raise and discipline a child you do not know even if you were the one that gave birth to the child. I understood that she was never there for me which opened the door to my defiance. Also, I witnessed too much. I believe the first time I met my dad I was about nine years old. Anytime we visited Alabama I would always go stay with my mom. The first time I remember meeting my mom, I was about five or six, however, on this visit when I met my dad, I was around nine years old.

He came to my mom's house to see me. He was an exceptionally clean cut and neat man. He told me that he was coming back the following day to take me shopping. My mom got me dressed, she did my hair and I sat by the door waiting for my dad to come and take me shopping that day. I sat by the door waiting on him for hours. Needless to say, he never showed up. I sat there looking and waiting until finally my mom told me to take my clothes off because he was not coming. The dysfunctional thing is the little girl within me remained by the door on into my adulthood. The little girl within wanted her daddy. I was forty years old before I was healed and delivered from her, but before my deliverance the desire to have my dad in my life caused me to seek acceptance through men even to the point of staying in abusive worthless relationships. I also will say this - because I desired to have a mother in my life, I *started calling older women "Mama" or looked at them as a mother figure because I was trying to fill a void. We never really understand how dysfunctional we are until we develop a relationship with God. The Word says in the book of Psalm 68:5(NIV) that God will be, **"A Father to the Fatherless."** It took a great deal of time for me to recognize that my mom nor my dad, could never in a million years, hold a torch to my Heavenly Father. I have been through a lot with my parents, but not just them, family period. Family will teach you how to have alligator skin when it comes to operating with church people, that is why I can never say I have been church hurt. The deepest hurt came from my family. In my opinion there is no hurt greater than family hurt. I am not downplaying a person being hurt by church people; that too is serious hurt, but for me, my family prepared me for the church.*

The sting of rejection has been my thorn but looking back over my life it was well worth the pain. There have been times I felt like no one wanted to be a part of my life in my family, and if truth be told, I still feel the same way. See, after a while the materialistic things get old. What I mean by this is there were members in my family that did things for me. They would show up when I needed certain things. They are the family members that wanted to be viewed as rescuers, and in the right heated moment they would remind me of everything

18

*they had done for me. They did things for me out of their own self-centeredness. Many people want the recognition that they so eagerly downplay. Hear me when I say, you must understand that everything happens for a reason. There is a reason why God allowed you to go through the pain you endured whether it was inflicted by family members, outsiders, or self-inflicted. There are times when we are out to get ourselves and do not realize it, otherwise known as "the demon within." If God had not allowed me to feel a sense of abandonment as it relates to family and some friends, I would have relied more on them and less on Him. This also included the men in my life as well. God had to allow pain to surface in my life to get my attention. Pain assisted in who I am today. It took seasons of pain for me to fully understand who God was and still is in my life. When family, friends and men walked out of my life God remained. Deuteronomy 31:8(ESV) helps us remember God's love. It says, **"He will not leave you nor forsake you."** I have found this to be the unadulterated truth. When I felt unloved, unheard, and unwanted by individuals in my life, God was there. Here is a saying that many people go by, "There's a light at the end of the tunnel." Well, that maybe true for the world, but for believers our Light goes through the tunnel with us. God is there even when we do not feel Him.*

My grandmother was a major part of my life from six months until I was fifteen, but she could not replace what I desired to have with my parents. As a child, having a relationship with my parents did not affect me because my grandmother and Charlotte family was all I knew. It was in my adult years that the emptiness began to surface and speak through my actions and choices. Pain can be so embedded in us that we begin to act out and not realize that we are acting out. It takes God's spiritual tilling and our yielding to the till for deliverance and healing to take place in those wounded areas of our lives. What many believers fail to realize is we can go through deliverance but still not be healed. Allowing God to do the tilling in our broken areas will usher in His healing. I had to go through major tilling.

I have been through a lot in my forty- seven years. I have been married twice. I went through physical, mental, and emotional abuse. If truth be told, I should not have gotten married to neither one of them. In my first marriage, I was young when I married him, he was my daughter's dad. I thought I was in love. I met him when I was fifteen, nothing or no one could keep me away from him. When I started a relationship with him, I was living with my dad and stepmom in Alabama. At the time of my living with them they were decent people, or it seemed; deception is always crouching at the door.

They allowed him to visit me, and he and I would sit in the living room and that is where our relationship began to develop.

Much of what I divulge about my life will be raw and to the point. Many problems arose while living with my dad and stepmom. I did not know back then who Jezebel and Ahab was, I had never heard of them. However, my dad and stepmom were the epitome of what those spirits looked like. Of course, I had some issues as well. I was rebellious and flat out defiant at times but overall, I was a fairly good girl. I believe when you are not loved by the people that are supposed to love you it can stir up something within you, and you may not fully understand at the time that it is really a cry for love and this is why you are acting out. Also, like I said earlier, materialistic things can never replace real love. My family would buy me things, but rarely did I hear," I love you." After things became too toxic between my dad, stepmom and I that is when I went to live with my mom. It was extremely difficult living with my stepmom. She was very jealous of my dad's and I relationship. I mean, it was not much of one and she made sure that nothing more progressed between the two of us. I remember sitting in the den with my dad watching television and after some time I went in the kitchen where my stepmom was to talk to her. When I sat down, I could tell she was aggravated. She told me to go back in the den with my dad because that was where I had been all day. That moment changed the stage on how I dealt with her. I knew if I was going to get along with her, I had to make her the center of my attention. She had to have complete control. She would do anything for me, but there was a wicked side to her that would manifest if she did not get her way. She could also be physically abusive not only to me, but my dad as well. I can recall her jumping on me in my room. She was fighting me like I was some random chic on the street and my dad had to rush in and break up the fight. I had to square up with her because she was not having any mercy on me. When my dad came in the room, he threw her on the bed and yelled, "she is a child!" My stepmom did not care, as most bullies don't. That was the only time I felt my dad's protection.

My dad was a lot different from her and was much easier to get along with, however, he was a habitual liar which made him dangerous. I carried the same lying spirit until I developed a real relationship with Christ, and then I came into the truth of the dangers of being a liar.

*John 8:44(NIV) teaches us that the devil is **"the father of lies."** Once I came into the true knowledge of Christ, I switched Fathers. Sad to say, many are still in a relationship with the wrong father. I will talk more about my dad and stepmom later in the book. God allowed them to be a part of why I had to endure seasons of pain.*

There were two key players Satan used to inflict serious damage in my life. So, not only is God allowing me to write this book to help others get through their painful seasons, but God is also healing me in some areas while writing this book. We can suppress areas in our lives and think we are healed, but the right triggers at the right time will expose unhealed pain. In one of my seasons of pain I went through a period where I was cussing people out.

The book of Ephesians 4:29(ESV) says:

"Let no corrupt talk come out of your mouths, but only such as is good for building up, as fits the occasion, that it may give grace to those who hear."

I allowed some serious corrupt talk to exit my mouth. What we think we have given to God to deal with will eventually surface if we have not fully given it to Him. Now I am going to transition you into what my life was like living with mom. My mom spoke these words to me, and I have never forgotten them. She said, "why hide what I'm doing from people when God see it?" This is one reason why I am an open book. God sees all and knows all, so why try to hide from people what you do? My mom and I still do not have a close relationship, but I love my mom. My mom did have some issues, but I will not speak against her. I honestly believe my mom had some unresolved hurt as it relates to her mother. She has never said anything to me about it. I just believe she spoke it through her actions, and this could be the reason why she kept me at bay. This is honestly my opinion; I am not totally sure why she chose to not fully embrace me as her daughter, but I love her, that's it that's all. As I think about her life and some of the things she has gone through, my heart breaks for her.

My mom and I had our run ins while I lived with her. I went as far as to pull a knife out on her. I fought her back when she slapped me in the face. We had our battles, but she is my mom, and I have grown to learn that you do not disrespect your mom no matter what she has done. She was a substance abuser. I personally believe it was a way for her to fill the emptiness within her she never put words to. Another way for her to fill the emptiness within her was to engage in abusive relationships. It was one relationship that she was involved in I witnessed firsthand. I tried to stop him a few times, but it only fueled his anger because he could not hit me for interfering. My great aunt would try to stop him, but she stopped getting involved after a while because my mom would not leave him alone. Plus, she was too old to deal with their fighting, or should I say, his fighting because what I witnessed with my mom was not fighting. One time I talked my mom into putting him out, but she let him come back that same night. I have learned that when you are trying to fill a void it becomes easy to accept detriment. Being rejected causes you to seek acceptance from people that you think love you, but in all actuality fake love is screaming loud through the way they treat you. Rejection will cause you to accept the appearance of love even if this love comes with a fist.

My mom had two sons by the man that she was married to. My youngest brother was murdered in a drug deal gone wrong. The death of my brother bothered me deeply - he and I had a pretty good relationship. I had a real sincere love for my youngest brother, he was a genuine person. The death of my youngest brother almost took my mom out. It was a lot for her to deal with seeing that she raised my brothers, plus there was a different kind of love she had for them. I had an interesting relationship with my oldest brother; he and I would argue a lot however, he would do anything in his power for me. He was my bodyguard. I personally believe my mom spoiled my oldest brother. It took some time and work, but he has developed into an amazing family man. Even though my oldest brother and I do not talk as much as we both may like, he has my heart. It was my brothers that put an end to my mom's boyfriend abusing her. They whipped him. They whipped him several times. One time they whipped him while he was sitting on the toilet. They kicked the door in and got him. One day my mom and him was sitting on the steps in front of an apartment complex called, "the hill" my oldest brother jumped out of the car and slapped him. My mom said, "what did you slap him for?" My brother replied, "I heard he was down here jumping on you." My mom said, "no he wasn't." My brother then replied, "well remember this the next time you jump on my Mama." Unfortunately, this is the price one might have to pay when they make the choice to abuse someone's mother. I have often wondered why I allowed myself to go through abuse, especially after witnessing my mom go through it. I honestly believe my wanting to be accepted opened me up to becoming a victim of abuse. The young man that I had started seeing at my dad and stepmom's house was now coming to see me at my mom's home. The rules were a little different at my mom's house. I had a lot more freedom to do what I wanted to do. She tried to watch us, but after a while we knew how to slip under the radar. Also, I had witnessed my mom go through too much, so any excessive discipline from her would have been out the question. It is hard to discipline a child that sees their parent's junk. Not only that, it is hard to raise a child that believes they have already been raised and is smart enough to detect when a parent is doing childish things. I eventually moved out of the home with my mom and moved in with my boyfriend and his mother; I was seventeen at the time.

What is sad is my parents never put up a real fight to make me leave out of the home with him. I later became pregnant with our daughter. He and I decided to share the news with my dad and stepmom and they both seemed happy, again mind you I was seventeen. The abuse I endured from him did not start right off, it was gradual. It was little fights that we had here and there that led to beatings. I remember us going to see my stepmom on her job and she saw that he was scratched up. She said, "Terra you can't be scratching him up like that! He is going to jump on you." She said this in front of him. What she did not realize, and I did not either, at the time, is that she opened the door and gave him permission to beat me. She never said, "don't put your hands on her." She said that by me scratching him it would lead to him jumping on me. She did not know what led up to the scratches; all she saw was that he was scratched, and the seeds of her words opened the door to abuse. I am not saying it was her fault that I was being abused; what I am saying is, we must be mindful of the words we release out of our mouth. Proverbs 18:21(NKJV) says,

"Death and life are in the power of the tongue."

We must watch what we say, and we must watch what people say to us. It is amazing how I went from being controlled, physically abused and emotionally abused by my dad and stepmom, and not feeling loved by my mom to being physically abused and controlled by my daughter's dad. The evil spirits within them ultimately became my master. It seemed like every time he and I would fight he would always hit me in the face. I guess the men who abuse their women do not understand that leaving bruises on her reflects who they are as men. Well, if he is demonically driven and does not have a real relationship with Christ, I guess he would not understand.

He hit me so many times in my face on my right cheekbone, that the bone was protruding out. I had gotten so used to being hit in the face that I did not realize my face was disfigured. I was working a third shift job at the time and a lady walked over to me, and said," you need to stop him from hitting you in the face; your face is disfigured." After she walked away, I got up and went to the bathroom and that is when I noticed my face. My right cheekbone was bigger than my left. You would have thought it would have been ammunition for me to leave but I did not. I went through so much abuse and him being unfaithful until I started having panic attacks. The entire time we were together he was sleeping with his children's mom. It is funny how a man can cheat with women who do not measure up to the woman he is with. He cheated on me with many different women including Caucasian women. He was so disrespectful that he would drive the Caucasian woman around knowing full well that it could get back to me, and it did. My stepmom was the first person to divulge the information, and it came secondly from two sisters that lived in my neighborhood. I remember one of the Caucasian women driving past our home and he immediately got in his car and followed her.

His children's mom and I was pregnant at the same time. Our girls are only a few months apart. He has allowed her to come in between every relationship he has had, but I do not fault her because he made the choice to keep messing around with her. I guess, my issue with her now is that she never understood her worth, and still does not; I didn't either when I was involved with him, but life has taught me my value. If I could say one thing to her it would be," Sis, let this man go. He has been married twice and still has not married you. Stop allowing him to rape your emotions. Give your life to the Lord and watch how you will begin to view things differently around you. If I wanted my daughter's dad back today, he would come and get me quicker than God can skin a melon!" My grandmother used to say that - Ha!

Okay, allow me to get back on track. He and I moved out of his mom's house and we moved into our own place, or should I say my place, because I was paying all the bills. After we moved in together the abuse and cheating did not stop but instead, got worse. After I got tired of being abused and cheated on, I left him and went to live with an uncle in Charlotte. On this particular morning he had been out all night so when he came home, he saw my and my daughter's clothes packed and sitting in the living room by the front door. He came in and asked me what was going on. I told him that I was leaving, he laughed and stepped over our clothes and went into the bedroom. Shortly after my uncle and aunt pulled up, and when he heard the car, he asked me who was outside. I replied, "My family is here." When he heard that his whole demeanor changed. My uncle and aunt came into the house to get my belongings, and before I got ready to leave, I went to the bedroom where he was, and he was sitting on the bed crying hard. I had never seen him in that state. I bent down to hug and kiss him, and he reached out to grab me, but I snatched away. I also noticed that he had cut his finger on the lamp we had in the bedroom. It was a deep cut, but I knew that I had to get out of there. Before we left, they took me and my daughter to visit my dad and stepmom. My dad received a call from my daughter's dad telling him to hold me there until he gets there. When he showed up, I went outside to talk to him. He was begging me to stay, but my mind was totally made up, plus, my uncle and aunt was not going to allow me to change it anyway.

When I arrived in Charlotte, I was still in contact with him. I do not know exactly how long I was in Charlotte, but I do know I was there for a while. He came to Charlotte to beg me to come back, but I was adamant about not leaving with him. He was so distraught that while he and I were outside he was crying in front of my uncle and some guys my uncle was talking to. At the time I did not realize it was subtle manipulation that I was experiencing from him through his tears. He eventually left, but about a month after he returned with his sister's then boyfriend. They had planned to abduct my daughter and I if I had opened the door. Before my uncle left for work, he told me not to open the door, and because I felt extremely uncomfortable, I was not going to anyway. My daughter's dad knocked on the door for a while before they decided to leave. We continued to stay in contact and that was how he was able to break me down. I agreed to go back with him, and this time he came with my dad. They say the third time is the charm. What is sad, is the man that was supposed to protect me drove my abuser to come and get me and his granddaughter. The evil spirits that was operating through them were relentless. But like I said earlier, my dad was never physically abusive - he was emotionally and verbally abusive. It was not hard for my daughter's dad to convince my dad. This is what you need to remember, evil spirits will come together within individuals to work against you; they do not have to like one another to do it. If they mutually agree to dislike you, they will work together until their mission is accomplished. When we returned to Alabama he and I got married shortly after. I wish that I could say the abuse and control stopped, but things became progressively worse after the newness of my returning wore off. He continued to cheat with his children's mother as well as other women. Allow me to back up. When I first started seeing him while living with my dad, we found out that he had his children's mom pregnant with their first child. My dad was not in agreement with me seeing him after we found out that she was pregnant. I was fifteen at the time and should not have been in a situation like that, however, the smoke soon cleared, and we continued seeing one another. Okay now, let's move forward. I hate that I remained in a relationship that consisted of abuse and infidelity. I remember one incident when we lived with his mom and he slammed me on the kitchen floor so hard that it knocked the breath out of me. His brother heard the commotion and saw me getting off the floor, and he said to him, "Man you're crazy! Hit me like that!" A fight broke out between the two of them. I had to run to their aunt's house to get help. I thank God his brother was there to help me. Unfortunately, it did not stop the abuse. I was kicked in the back while walking down the stairs and I was pregnant at the time. There was a time he hit me so hard in my ear the doctor said I had a bruise on the inside of my ear. What made me go to the emergency room was because after he hit me, I was unable to turn my head on the side I was hit on (my left side.) One day we were riding in the car and I saw this guy that I knew; I did not speak to him - all I did was look at him and my daughter's dad hit me in my chest so hard that a knot formed immediately. On another occasion he beat me with a broom stick so bad that it broke (I am talking about the thick broom sticks we used back in the day.) My leg was swollen and badly discolored. When I saw it, I screamed at him, "Look what you've done to my leg!" The bruising and swelling must have frightened him because he went to the pharmacy to get ointment, but not only did he have the ointment, he also had apology gifts as a peace offering. I have plenty of stories of the abuse I endured but I will conclude with these. I had become so tired of being beat that I was contemplating taking his life. Someone had given me some embalming fluid. It was for my nail polish. It was said that if you put a drop or two in your nail polish it would help your nails grow. My advice to those of you reading this book is please do not try this at home. If you put too much embalming fluid in nail polish it hurts like crazy, and you would have to be a little demented to try something like this anyway.

Okay, let's get back focused. I wanted to use the embalming fluid to kill him, but God had other plans for my life, so He got me out of that abusive marriage. Mark tells us in 10:9(NIV),

"Therefore, what God has joined together, let no one separate."

Some of these marriages God did not put together, we did. God does not approve of any kind of abuse, and He definitely, does not want His children remaining in a marriage that consist of it. This is why we must use wisdom when listening to religious people that tell us to remain in this kind of marriage. I asked this guy who I conversed with through social media, who was adamant against divorce, if he believed a woman or even a man should leave the marriage if they were being abused. His reply was, "no." He said the individual should call the police, but they should not leave the marriage. I then said, "What if it is your Mama? You don't think she should leave?" His reply was, "no." He said God called us to be martyrs and if a believer dies at the hands of their spouse that is their way of paying homage to God. That was some of the most unhinged asinine buffoonery I had ever heard in my life. When leaders in the body give this kind of advice, they are sending some believers back home to face death row. It is imperative that we seek God's face when we find ourselves in violent marriages. Yes, God can restore a marriage however, there are people that the enemy will use, and they come in spouse form. That is why we must be cautious of who we marry. At the time when I was married to my daughter's dad, I had no clue of who God was calling me to be, nor was I thinking about being anyone God wanted to use. I finally left him and returned to Charlotte. There comes a time when you must want more for yourself; sometimes it takes longer for some people to understand that. There is more to life than being controlled and abused. I asked my dad and stepmom if they could drive me to Charlotte, and they agreed.

Allow me to give you the set up on how everything transpired, and how I was able to get away from him. The day I was leaving, my stepmom came to help me pack. As we were packing, I looked out the window and noticed my daughter's dad racing towards our home.

Someone had to have called him on his job and informed him that I was planning to leave that day. The only people that knew was my dad and stepmom. I have always believed that my dad was responsible for him finding out. I do not think my dad made the call himself, however, I do believe he could have put someone up to do it. When he walked into the house, he saw me, and my daughter's things packed in the living room. Shortly after he arrived, my stepmom said that she had to leave. At the time her and my dad were having marital issues. It was as if she received an epiphany about my dad and needed to go see what was going on with him, because she made the comment that she had her own issues in her marriage. Now that I think about it, she might have been the one who told him. I mean, who would leave the person they claim to love with their abuser right after they just got caught trying to leave? After she left, he made me get in the car with him and we drove to a nearby wooded area. He told me that he was going to kill me and dump my body in the woods. He said, "No one will be able to find you in the woods." My reply was, "Allow me to ask God to forgive me for my sins so that I can go to heaven." I was just that tired of being abused. So, if it had to be death that got me out of my marriage then I was ready to die.

Let's have a sidebar. My dad never confronted him about abusing me, and in some strange way I think he may have thought I deserved it. I really believe he wanted him to kill me. My dad and I was conversing in 2016 or 2017 and he said, "I had people to tell me that he was jumping on you, and I said, 'I ain't messing with that fool! He crazy! He will shoot you!'" We laughed at what he said, but his words left a scar on me. A father should be willing to die for his daughter. What makes this so sad is I am his only child. The only time I felt protected by my dad was when my stepmom attacked me. I recall some girls from High School wanting to jump on me. They came in car loads at the place I mentioned earlier called "the hill." Someone called my dad and stepmom and told them what was going on. My stepmom came with her gun; by the time she arrived we were at a nearby restaurant however it was still a little heated. She jumped out of her car and shot in the air and of course that calmed the situation down. She told me that my dad said he was not coming, and that she could go, so he stayed in the bed. What real father would remain in the bed while his daughter is about to get jumped on by a group of girls? I will tell you, one that was being used by the enemy. I believe my dad and my stepmom's assignment was to inflict so much pain on me that I would not ever come into the full knowledge of God because I would be filled with so much hate. I believe they were the Devil's spiritual handlers for my life. They were the ones who willfully drove daggers into my back without any remorse.

Some people make it easy for the Devil to use them. They open themselves up to the Devil to be in full control of how he works against the people he is after. I honestly believe my dad hates me; maybe he hates me because I am a reminder of the sin he committed with my mom. I have asked God numerous times why He allowed me to be birthed through him. I have finally come to understand that it was never about him; it was about the call and purpose on my life. The reason I do not hate them is because what God has called me to do is too great and hating them will only allow the enemy to win.

Now, let's get back to the situation with my daughter's dad. He decided not to kill me, and we drove back home. We sat and talked for a while, but he had to return to work. In a final attempt to control me, he asked for all the rings he purchased me. He knew that I loved my jewelry, so he thought that if he took my rings that would make me not try to leave again after he went back to work. After he headed out, I was getting ready to leave out and go to a friend's house to ask for help, but something told me to wait because he was going to call when he got to work. This man went back to work after catching me trying to attempt to leave for a second time. I do not care what anybody says, I now know that something was the Holy Ghost. I did not know much about the Holy Ghost at that time but looking back I know that it was Him guiding me.

As I waited the phone finally rung and it was him. He told me that we would work things out when he got off work. I agreed, but my mind was made up, I was leaving one way or the other. When I hung up with him, I immediately ran out the house to a friend's house and asked for help. She jumped up got her keys and we drove back to my house and we picked up where me and my stepmom left off. Mind you, my stepmom never called to see if I was okay. Once we were finished packing, we started loading up her car. As we were loading up, we saw a guy that lived in the neighborhood and asked him to help us, after the car was loaded, she and I went to pick up my daughter, his brother's wife was keeping her that day. Once I got my daughter we headed to my dad's house. When we pulled up at my dad and stepmom's house, I got out and went into the house my dad was sitting in the kitchen. I asked him if he could still drive me to Charlotte - he said he would, but I had to give him seventy dollars for gas. Listen, my dad charged me! Why would a dad make his daughter, who is trying to escape her abusive husband pay for gas? Mind you, my daughter witnessed a lot of my abuse. This is what she said: "When I get big, I'm going to kill my daddy." You would have thought my dad would have done everything in his power to help me out of my abusive marriage. He should have given me money instead of asking me for my money. This is the reason why I believe my dad secretly hates me. You would think I was this bad person. I was fifteen when my dad came to get me from my grandmother. I have done what many teenagers have done. I am not trying to excuse any of my behavior. I stole, I had sex, and one time I got drunk. These are all forgivable things.

Let me expound on one of the things I did. My stepmom cleaned houses and she would take me with her. I told you earlier that I loved jewelry. I stole a necklace out of a house and a ring out of another house she worked at; both items were retrieved from me but this is the kicker - Instead of keeping it in the home and dealing with it privately they told others which got back to the high school I attended. Also, there was a time that I got so angry with them that I slashed my arm with a razor (I still have the scars to prove it.) Instead of them dealing with it in the home, somehow the kids at the High School found out before I got to school the next day. Anything I did they made sure that everyone in town knew. It was as if they were intentionally trying to destroy my life. We lived in Dadeville, Alabama and a word spoken there could spread quicker than a disease. I do understand now why I had to go through it. Who God has called me to be is connected to what I went through. I had to go through a serious healing process as I developed a real relationship with Christ. Okay, let me shift back. I cannot remember what we talked about on the drive to Charlotte. I was just elated that I was finally getting away again and I was not going back this time no matter what. I was conversing with a childhood friend and I divulged to her what I was going through, and she let my daughter and I live with her. I did not bother to ask my Charlotte family, because the uncle that allowed me to live with him the first time I left my daughter's dad said, that if I went back to him and it did not work out I could not come back to live with him again, so I knew that door was closed. I understand the point he was trying to make, however, that is not how family should operate. I am not saying be a fool and keep running to a person's aid who really does not want to change, however what I am saying is we should not write family off, especially when some of the ones doing the writing has had issues themselves. This same uncle had a cocaine addiction at one point in his life, and the ones that loved him did not write him off. This uncle was never the easiest to get along with at times, but I still would have thought he would have had a little more empathy. That is how it is, when people come out of their situation, they tend to have a critical eye on other individuals that are having a little harder time coming out of theirs.

I have learned throughout my journey that everything happens for a reason, and the people involved had their own personal role in the journey of my life. When I arrived in Charlotte it felt like a weight was lifted off my shoulders. It was sad watching my dad and stepmom leave but I was free! I remember waking up the next day and reality hit me like a ton of bricks - I was no longer in Alabama and I was not going back. My emotions were all over the place but again, I was free, I was free! I did not have to live like a caged animal anymore. Allow me to say this, it bothers me greatly to hear people say it is the woman's fault for not leaving her abuser. What most people do not understand is the woman's mind has been trained and conditioned by her abuser, in many cases. The woman's mind has been molded and conditioned by her abuser to think the way he wants her to think. The abuser will start by implementing fear which is then followed by control and manipulation. He will also strip her mind because if he can dominate her thoughts, he can force her into controlled submission. Many women operate like this daily and do not know that they are being controlled. The abuser will always show who is the dominate one. But let's be realistic, there are some women who are the abusers as well. This book is in no way intended to make men out to be villains. I understand that men too are abused, but many of them are not as open as women, so we do not hear their stories as much, which causes a lot of men to suffer in silence.

The signs of an abuser can be detected early in most relationships, we miss it because our emotions and feelings override the red flags. Our emotions and feelings will slip in and silence the warning signs that are prevalent. We also must be mindful of insecurities and low self-esteem because an abuser can detect what we try to mask and play off of it. They will use insecurity and low self-esteem as a tool to keep their victims lured in. Another tool an abuser will use is beatings. Beatings are a way to ensure that the individual will not leave even if they have an out, because beatings symbolically speaks death. Remember, I said the abuser will train and condition the individual's mind. Many times, the abuser will study their victims; this is how they gain control. They will study the person long enough to learn what the individual does not recognize about themselves and use it as ammunition. Even though I was a victim, it was not in God's plan that I die or stay in an abusive marriage. Allow me to park here for second. It is essential that fathers are in their daughter's lives. As strange as it may sound, a father is his daughter's first boyfriend. A father sets the stage for what his daughter should require in a man. Many women as well as (myself) tolerated broken dysfunctional relationships, because we had a broken dysfunctional relationship with our dad. I wish that I could say that I learned my lesson about toxic relationships after being with my daughter's dad, but unfortunately, I did not.

I went on to engage in other unhealthy relationships, yes, four more beautiful children conceived out of broken relationships. I mentioned earlier that I have been married twice. Well, to be fair my second marriage showed me that there are men who are great providers, and I also believe he loved me with the love he understood to be love. He is a wonderful Father to his son which is my youngest, and he was a good man; I simply believe he was not ready to father someone else's children, which was an ingredient for the decline of our marriage. It takes the love of Christ to love someone else's children like they are your very own. Many will do it in public, however in private you will see the real creature behind the mask. God warned me not to marry him; He saw what I was not capable of seeing at the time. I saw the consistency that he possessed not the dysfunction masked behind the consistency. God showed me that my consistency and His consistency was different. God said I was looking at physical consistency in my life, but if he wasn't spiritually consistent with Him then he couldn't be consistent in every aspect of my life. He and I both had inner undealt with issues that we tried to pass off as love. These unchecked issues could become explosive when a problem between the two of us surfaced. He was never physically abusive, however, there was a lot of emotional and verbal abuse between the both of us. God was trying to spare me of this. God knew that he and I were not ready to be married because of the hurtful experiences from our past. I did not adhere to the warning signs, so I had to endure the heartache and pain that came along with my disobedience. I really must take a lot of the ownership in this situation because I knew better. I understood what God was showing me however, I chose to ignore it. It will behoove you to never ignore God's warnings. My two older boys' dad is a factor in their lives. I believed I was in love with him. As I grew in my relationship with Christ, He showed me what being in love consisted of. God showed me I could not be in love with anyone that was not connected to Him, because they did not know how to display the love that would cause me to fall in love.

God showed me that I was in lust not love. I was in a fantasy relationship. A fantasy relationship is a relationship the individual has created in their own mind. There is nothing produced out of a fantasy relationship but perhaps children, and this would entail what the relationship was really based off of. I was not in love with him, I was in love with his sex. It's funny how our mind will play tricks on us. There was some physical abuse in this "fantasyship," but not much. I met him before I had a genuine relationship with Christ. I remember getting on my knees and begging God to remove the feelings I had for him. I said to God that if I were His child then why would he allow me to have feelings for a man that did not feel the same for me. A few days after the prayer my feelings began to change. I no longer saw him the same. The hold he had on me had diminished. He never intended to make me his woman. I was the "something to do" that he ended up having feeling for but never was intending to have a serious relationship with at all. I was that diamond in the rough. When a diamond is found it might be covered in dirt however, it is still a diamond. Some men see this when it is too late. My third son's dad is the epitome of a shirk; he is the reason why women need to wait on the Lord. Lust will set you up to be lured in by sinister individuals. Its assignment is to deceive you into believing that you can build a life with a person who in fact does not have a life. I will have to take ownership in this situation, well I take ownership in all my broken relationships because I played apart. I allowed a lot of what happened to me to happen because I did not understand my worth, so, I will not place blame on any of these men. I started dealing with this man knowing full well he had kids by different women before I entered the picture, and he was not doing right by some of the mothers. You would have thought I would have told him to get the heck on, but I allowed his smooth corny lines to seduce me, and we conceived my third son.

After I had my son, I was very fatigued, so he came over to help me with him (at the time we were not together.) Wait, let me share this. When he found out I was pregnant he tried to make me have an abortion, but I was adamant about not killing my child. I had already had an abortion a year earlier, and the one thing they do not tell you is how it messes with your mind after you murder your child, because that is what it is, murder. It took me repenting and asking God to forgive me before I was really healed, and even though I am healed and forgiven I still think about my baby. I still wonder at times if it was a boy or a girl. So, no he was not about to force me into another abortion. He even tried to manipulate me by telling me his mom said he did not need any more children. I had to remind him that his mom did not pay the bills at my house, so she could not tell me what to do, however, due to fatigue he would come over some nights and help me with my son. I was sleeping on the couch in the living room while he and my son slept in my bed. That quickly changed into us being in the room together and then him moving in with me shortly after. It is amazing how we settle for less, this man moved in with me. What's wrong with that picture? But anyway, when he first moved in, we were trying to have a relationship, but I later found out that he was still involved with his other children's mother. After some time, he left me to go back with one of the other mothers. While I was working, he moved his belongs out - how cowardly was that? But this was what he did, he played musical chairs with his children's moms. I must say I was devastated when I got home and seen all his junk gone, and to make things worse he came back trying to explain why he left. That is like breaking into someone's home, and later going back trying to explain why you robbed them. Man!!!!! Get outta here!!! While he was living with her, he was still communicating with me, and I am sure some of his other children's moms as well.

After a while, things began to go sour between the two of them, and he asked if he could come back to live with me. I allowed him, yep I know, crazy, huh? But check this out - the second time was worse than the first. He came back in an abusive manner, he hit me. It was only once, but it was one time too many. I was not going to allow this man to hit me. It would have been ugly for him, because I had made up in my mind that I was not going to allow another man to hit me. After he left the second time, I did not deal with him anymore. He was in my son's life briefly, but he was not consistent which caused major problems with my son. Even my second husband dropped the ball as it pertained to my third son (that is why it is imperative that you have an understanding with your spouse when it comes to children that are not theirs biologically. This is something that needs to be discussed before marriage. His dad tried to reconnect a few times, but I was growing in my relationship with God, so my eyes were opened to the kind of man he really was. He does not have anything to do with my son anymore. One day we were having words and I told him that he will always glean from someone else's land, because he has neglected to take care of his own seeds. I have decided to leave him in the hands of God. Ladies, we must own our part in pairing with men who do not understand our worth. We must ask ourselves, what is it in us that would allow us to be with men that we know are not good for us even while in our filth.

Men, I am not leaving you out. Many of you have been hurt by the women in your lives. There are women who are living the harlot life, and have destroyed good men, or almost destroyed them. Some men are hurting and are causing hurt to women because of what a woman has done to them. Just like a woman the man must seek the face of God as it pertains to his soulmate. Having the wrong rib in your cage can cause physical and spiritual problems. Here is the thing, there is always some kind of warning signs. We miss it because our insecurities and low self-esteem are shouting louder than the small still voice

within us.

Chapter 2
My Pain, My Daughter

I wish that I could say that I did not have to deal with my tormentors after I left Alabama, but the devil will not allow you to freely walk away without a fight. I was soon about to find myself caught in his web again. The enemy is always lurking. 1 Peter 5:8(NIV) tells us to, **"Be alert and of sober mind. Your enemy the devil prowls around like a roaring lion looking for someone to devour."**

I received a call from my dad asking if they could get my daughter for the summer and I agreed. When my dad and step mom arrived to get my daughter, I was smart enough to put in writing that she was only supposed to go for the summer; I was even smart enough to have my friend's mom to sign as a witness, but what I did not do was have a copy made for my personal records and protection. I allowed my dad and stepmom to take the written copy without having a copy made for myself. That was the worst mistake I have ever made in my life. Had I known that would be the last time I would have my daughter living with me I would not have ever let her go with them. I trusted them to love her enough not to try to hurt me through her. When they arrived in Alabama that is when my world stood still. My daughter's dad took her from my dad and stepmom and there was not anything they could do about it, nor was there anything the police could do because he was her dad. I am not quite sure if what I wrote on paper would have even mattered since it was her dad that took her. I was ignorant to all of this when I agreed to let her go. It is imperative that we understand State Laws and the rights we have. My daughter's dad had every right to take her and there was not anything I could do.

I think about the time when I was in Alabama and my dad said that I should have another baby and let him, and my stepmom have my daughter. I laughed it off, but I now believe that the three of them planned to take my daughter as a ploy to get me to come back to Alabama. They might not have come together as a team, but I do believe they did it for their own personal gain. It would not shock me though, if my dad had a conversation with my ex-husband. I am sure my dad knew the rights that my ex-husband had; he also knew that I did not know my rights at the time. I believe he may have set the stage for my ex-husband to take my daughter and then sat back and played the victim. Deception runs deep in my dad. I did not fully understand this at the time. I thought they just wanted to run my life, now I know that it was something much more sinister going on. At the time I did not realize how serious all of this was. I thought I was going to get my daughter back. I believed things just needed to run its course. I believed my dad and stepmom were really going to help me. It is sickening how deceiving they were. They got a lawyer, and we took it to court. My dad told me to tell the lawyer I wanted them to have custody. He told me once they got custody, they would give her back to me because it would be hard for me to take her out of Alabama, seeing that I did not live there anymore. I was desperate to get my daughter back, so I agreed.

The first time we went to court I was prepped by the Lawyer, my dad and stepmom on what to say. I do not remember a lot of what happened at the first hearing; I do remember before going to court my stepmom told me to put salt in my shoes. I did not know that was witchcraft at the time. Well, whatever the salt was supposed to do, it did not, because I still left Alabama without my daughter. Before we had the second court hearing my dad told me that they were no longer going to pay for the lawyer. They asked me to ask an aunt of mine to continue paying the lawyer fee. I did, and she declined. This aunt could not stand them, so she was not going to assist in anything they had going on even at the risk of hurting me. For me alone I am sure she would have helped, but because she knew that my dad and stepmom was the reason, I was going through this she did not want anything to do with it. I remember right before going to court the second time my dad and stepmom got into a physical fight in the bathroom. It was so doltish I cannot remember what led up to it. I was not shocked because they were always fighting. Anytime my stepmom did not get her way she resorted to verbal or physical attack. They finally got it together and we left for the court hearing. When I was called to the stand it literally felt like I was in Hell being interrogated by Satan and his minions. As I was being questioned by my ex-husband's lawyer, I watched the lawyer that was supposed to defend me have a seat in the audience. I could tell by her facial expression she knew things were going to go awry. The male Judge that presided over our case seemed to hate me. He said, "Mrs. Gray, why don't you want your daughter?" I said, "Sir, I do." He then said, "I have a statement here saying that you wanted to give custody to your parents." I tried to explain to him that I was told to say it by the Lawyer, my dad and stepmom, but he was not hearing anything I had to say. I was later told that an aunt of my ex-husband was there, and she operated in witchcraft, and that is why things transpired the way it did. Whether that was true or not I am not sure, but I do know that he was awarded temporary custody. At the time he was washing cars for a living. I had two jobs, but he was still awarded custody of my daughter.

Allow me to stop right here and share something with you all. My dad had a root put on him. The woman he was committing adultery with put it on him in more ways than one. I went to a psychic with my stepmom, and she told her that my dad had a root on him. The way my dad's behavior had shifted, it was something diabolical going on there with him. He had started back drinking heavy, it was like what was on him wanted to kill him. As I reflect on the day that I went to see the psychic with my stepmom, there were two ladies there at the house. One of the ladies was sitting in the living room when we walked through the door, and once I saw her, I felt this creepy weird feeling. She looked like something out of a serious horror movie. We went in the kitchen, sat at the table and that is where the readings commenced. My stepmom went so far as to go into the woman my dad was seeing laundry room and got a pair of her underwear and buried them. She was doing what she was instructed to do by the psychic. I know many of you are wondering how she got in the laundry room. Well, some of the houses laundry rooms back then were connected to the outside of the house. The door was unlocked and that is how she retrieved the underwear. So yes, my stepmom operated in witchcraft too. I did not understand how dangerous witchcraft was at the time. I was going along for the ride. I have repented for all involvement I had. The psychic spoke a word to me as well while I was there. I did not know that all of this was tied to witchcraft at the time I chose to participate. I told you earlier that my dad and stepmom carried the Jezebel and Ahab spirit. The sad part is I was blind to all of this at the time, and plus I still trusted them. I honestly believed they were on my side.

I returned to Charlotte wounded. It felt like all of life in me was being sucked out of me. How do you just plot to take a child from their mother? It is not like I was an unfit mother, even though my stepmom told my daughter that I burned her with an iron on her leg to punish her. I would iron on the bed because I did not have an ironing board. I placed the iron on the floor, and she backed up to the iron. My stepmom and ex-husband also told my daughter that I hated her and did not want her. It was not that I did not want my daughter, I did not have the money to pay a lawyer, so I foolishly gave up the fight, plus, they had already awarded temporary custody to her dad. To tell a child such things about their mother is villainous. My dad plays all sides but will sit back and act like he is the mediator. My dad is on the person's side he is talking to at the time - he is the epitome of a jelly back. My daughter is twenty-nine years old and married with three girls of her own. My dad and stepmom have brainwashed her to the point that she does not know what to believe. She knows that they are liars and troublemakers, but these are the people that helped raise her in *a sense, so there is still some trust there even though she knows they can be scandalous. I could have done more for my daughter. I must admit I dropped the ball in some areas, but I love her, and I know that God will heal and restore what the canker worms have eaten. I honestly believe the devil was using them to try and destroy me. The devil knew something I did not know. He knew that I had a call on my life; he was trying to cause so much calamity that I would hate them and never fully get to know God. I was supposed to be so full of hate, unforgiveness, bitterness and anger that I allowed it to become my master versus getting to know the real Master. But this is the thing, I refuse to allow devils, or should I say the working of the devil to stop the flow of my blessings. I had to forgive them so that I could be healthy spiritually, mentally and physically.*

Walking around with unforgiveness within you can take a toll on your body. I know individuals right now that are battling health issue after health issue because they choose to not forgive. Many times, our body goes through physical pain because it is not equipped to take on the baggage that we are so willing to carry around. I have an aunt that hates my oldest brother's guts and to this day she has chronic back pain. The unforgiveness spirit is lodged in her back and is wrapped around her spine. She has personally told me that she hated my brother and has wished death on him, but she professes to be a follower of Jesus Christ. What she fails to realize is her body will be a playground for demons until she makes the choice to forgive. So many professing believers are sick and have died because they have chosen not to forgive. Making the choice to forgive is for you, because forgiveness can hold the spirit of death back. I was forty-four years old before I really began to see the damage my dad had done to me, and he was one of the ones I cussed out. I had suppressed so much of my pain that I exploded, and he felt the effects of it. That is why it is important that we give our pain to God. I wanted a relationship with my dad so bad that I ignored all the warning signs, even when they were crystal clear. It is amazing how the people that are supposed to love and take care of you can be so diabolical, however, I must remember what Ephesians 6:12(NIV) says,

"For our struggle is not against flesh and blood, but against the rulers, against the authorities, against the powers of this dark world and against the spiritual forces of evil in the heavenly realms.

God allowed me to be birthed through my dad. I am his only child, so why do this to me? Well, if I believe what Ephesians tells me it was never about my family, they were simply vessels being used. As the scales fell off my eyes I still desired to have a relationship with my dad and stepmom, but because they have so many open doors to be utilized by the enemy it has made it too difficult to have any kind of connection with them. We think because we are believers, we got to always make things right. If God is in it, of course. But what I have learned is, you cannot make things right with a demon. When the demon is in operation the individual has no control. Many people are used willingly, and then there are others who are used unwillingly. I wholeheartedly believe my dad and stepmom were willing vessels for the enemy to be used.

There has been a hit out on my life since birth and that is why things happened the way it did. Satan sent out his demons to house family members, so-called friends, men and sideliners because he caught a glimpse. Satan understood that he could not kill me, so he went after my mind. He thought if he could use them to help in the destruction of my mind that it would ultimately destroy me. I was supposed to be a basket case, but God!!! As I look back on my life and what I had to endure, I can see the fingerprints of God even while I was rolling around in my own mess. That is why we must understand why it is necessary to go through our painful seasons. Pain helps to develop who you are. When we make the decision to yield to our pain it ushers in deliverance and healing. Think about this, if we did not have pain, we would not know we had a problem. Pain helps to detect the underlined symptoms. In most cases before we go to see a doctor, there must be the presence of pain. Once we explain the location of the pain to the doctor that is when he or she can assess the nature of the problem. When we are honest about our pain that is when God can heal the symptoms. Most people do not want to go through painful seasons because it forces them to have to look at themselves in the mirror, and some of us do not like the person staring back at us.

Pain will cause you to have to examine yourself, and that is why some people try to bypass pain. If it were not for my seasons of pain, I would not have the relationship with Christ that I do. My pain ushered in His presence. My pain ushered in His peace. My pain helped me understand the attributes of God, while He was teaching me the attributes of me. Jeremiah 15:18(NIV) says,

"Why is my pain unending and my wound grievous and incurable?"

When we go through seasons of pain it can seem never ending. Focusing too much on the pain and not the healer of our pain will deceive us into believing we will not make it through our painful seasons, which can cause us to murmur and complain.

Murmuring and complaining only prolongs the process. The wounds that have been inflicted can bleed profusely, and any unhealed wounds can cause even greater pain. It is mandatory that we trust God during the healing process. The enemy wants us to focus on the pain because when we focus on the pain it can trick us into believing the pain is greater than God.

Chapter 3
My Pain, My Parents, My Family

We do not have a choice what family we will be born into. It can be very disheartening when you do not feel love from the ones that came together and birthed you. I must say not all my family members are sinister. I believe that my dad and stepmom are the only vessels that the Devil tried to use for his plan. Now, I do believe other family member were distractions, but I would not go so far as to call them sinister. A few of them played a serious part in some of my hurt, but it has not been anything like what I had to endure with my dad and stepmom. It takes deep rooted evil to treat a person how my dad and stepmom treated me. I would expect that from outsiders, but I have not had any outsiders to mishandle me like they did. My mom may have given me to my grandmother to raise, but as I stated earlier, I believe my mom had her own hurt and pain that she never voiced. I mean, she was given to her aunt to be raised by while her mother raised my mom's other three siblings, that can be painful. It makes you wonder what was so different about you that made them not want to deal with you.

Again, my mom has never expressed her feelings as it pertains to my grandmother. I have never heard her say anything negative about my grandmother, but that does not negate the fact that she was not hurting. That could be the reason for the addiction and the destructive relationships. Now, I understand why my daughter is so unbalanced as it relates to our relationship. It could be that she felt rejected, but I would never reject or not want any one of my children, but it is hard to prove that when so much evil has been spoken to my daughter. All I can do now is put it in God's hands. She is a grown woman with a mind of her own, and I understand that her mind has been contaminated, however, when healing and deliverance is really desired by the Lord, that is when He will begin to help us decipher through the truth and the lies. Now, I was not perfect, and I could have handled some things differently, but I never gave my daughter away, she was stolen from me.

As I stated earlier, I have never felt genuine love from my family, but I honestly do not believe it was ever meant for me to fit in. God had a different plan for my life, and I could not become too comfortable with my family because it would have stifled my spiritual growth, so God had to keep me feeling unaccepted by them. Yes, even with me believing my dad and stepmom were driven by evil spirits, and some of my other family members were major distractions, I still believe God allowed everything to happen so that His glory would illuminate off His investment, which is me. Romans 8:18 (ESV) says,

"For I consider that the suffering of this present time is not worth comparing with the glory that is to be revealed to us."

No matter what I have had to endure God's glory has been and will continue to be revealed in my life. That is why I hold no grudges, bitterness, hatred, resentment or unforgiveness. God's glory is worth too much to allow the devil to snuff out God's plan for my life.

Chapter 4
My Pain, My Marriages

I know I have talked about my marriages; however, I feel compelled to delve a little deeper. It is so important for a dad to be a factor in his daughter's life. It can help steer her decision making as it pertains to her choice in men. Now, there are some females that are going to do what they want to do, but that still does not negate the fact that girls need their dads. When the dad is absent in his daughter's life or just does not put in the extra time, it can cause her to search for the attention she desires from her dad through other men. This does not necessarily mean she is a whore. Some females are looking for the love they desire to feel from their dads. As I reflect on my past relationships, I always engaged with guys that tried to control me or did control me. I believe this stemmed from the befouled authority that my dad tried to lord over me. A lot of the time women will seek out men who remind them of their dad whether good or bad. In my first marriage my ex-husband was extremely controlling and abusive. My dad was never physically abusive, but he did try to control my life, even through manipulation. You would have thought I would run from any signs of control, but I ran straight to it. In some defiled way I guess I believed he loved me because he was willing to control and fight me if I did not do what he asked. This is how Satan deceives women. He will have you thinking that the man must love you because he is willing to get physical. Ladies, black eyes, swollen lips, a bloody nose and broken bones does not convey love, it speaks hate. He has got to hate you as well as himself, and it also shows that he has low self-esteem and insecurities. I have learned that most men have an inner little boy within them that will act up when they cannot have their way. The little boy mostly shows up at home because that is his territory. Occasionally, it will pop up outside the home, but it is safest in the home because that is where it goes undetected from other people.

Some women believe that they are dealing with a frustrated, angry man, and some are, however, if you study him like he has probably studied you, you will detect when you are dealing with the man versus the boy. It will take him recognizing it and seeking healing and deliverance from God. Many men are angry with their mothers, and because of this they take their pain and frustration out on women. This too requires the help of God. My second marriage was done out of my own disobedience. I mentioned earlier that God warned me not to marry him, but his consistency overpowered what God was trying to show me. I had never experienced real consistency from any other tangible man in my life. The only thing my dad was consistent in doing was trying to destroy my life. So, when I saw pure consistency from my second husband it won me over despite the warnings God was trying to show me. But having consistency without spiritual substance is a recipe for disaster. We were unequally yoked, but I did not see it at the time, or should I say, I did not want to see it. I was caught up in church and not the Kingdom, so I did not focus on the religious spirit that was prevalent within him. Also, I was in love with being married not what it took to remain married. Many women are in marriages because they wanted to be married more than they wanted the man, so when a problem arises they look to get married again versus working it out with the one they are married to, because her emotions are tied to being married. She fights to be married but does not put up the same fight to remain married because her heart is not with the man, it is with being married. My second husband was a good man but when you are finally Kingdom having a good man that is not willing to go higher in his relationship with the Lord can stifle many things.

Ladies, you will need more than just a good man. Listen to what Proverbs 18:22(NKJV) tells us:

"He who finds a wife finds a good thing

And obtains favor from the Lord".

Sisters listen, the favor is on us, but at times we are sharing our favor with men God never told us to marry; we married them out of our own personal insecurity. There are so many women who are stuck in a miserable marriage, and they are waiting for the man to die so they can obtain freedom; that is why it is imperative that we adhere to the warning signs God is showing us. I thought by him being consistent and at least going to church we would make it. I was wrong. Now, God can do a work in broken marriages however, it is wise that we listen to our Father. It will spare us the heartache and headache.

Also, it is especially important that he is ready to take on another man's child(ren). There are men who will love the woman but only tolerate her child(ren). You must watch men who eagerly disciplines your child(ren) but hardly shows love. That is why it is important that you know how he was raised. Ladies, you must ask questions. Men, you must ask questions as well. Some women do not want to be bothered with someone else's child(ren), which makes their toleration level extremely low. You need to know if their mom and dad was active in their life before you make a choice to be with the individual. Allow me to say this, just because a parent or both parents were not involved in their life, that does not mean it is a deal breaker; it simply helps you gauge how to be in prayer. Also, you must watch how the individual interacts with your child(ren) and be in prayer as well as discerning because some individuals know how to mask their annoyance very well. Allow me to say this, it is imperative for women to pray and ask God for a husband she desires and one that God desires for her. Yes, the woman is to be found by the man however, as she waits to be found she should make her request known.

The word says in, Jeremiah 29:12(NIV),

"Then you will call on me and come and pray to me, and I will listen to you."

We must be in prayer when it comes to who God wants us to marry. Just because the man thinks he has found a good thing, does not mean we have to be found by him. Men, many of you are having spiritual chest pains because you did not seek the Lord for your rib, and now the rib you chose is making it difficult for you to breathe. You must know that you know it is God leading you to the person. You do not want anyone that has two different personalities, and you do not want to marry a person that is not prepared to love your child(ren) as their own. Do not play with God's warnings, adhere to them the first time. Also, do not allow your feelings and emotions to override God's still small voice, and sometimes His voice is like a mighty rushing wind and we still ignore His warnings. There are those of us who need to repent for our disobedience. We must acknowledge our part in the situation so that we can move on.

Chapter 5
My Pain, My Change

When I yielded to my seasons of pain, that is when I began to grow. We must yield to our pain, but not allow our pain to master us. Ecclesiastes 3:1(KJV) reminds us that,

> **"To everything there is a season, and a time to every purpose under the heaven".**

It is mandatory that we go through our painful seasons. Now listen to me closely, go through your season of pain, but do not allow the spirit of pity to consume you. Pity is sent to stagnant your growth. Also, watch the people that pity you, because if the people in your camp or around the surrounding areas of your camp pity you they do not see any more for your life than you do. You will need pushers not individuals who are willing to assist in your stagnation. The pity spirit has seized many professing believers. They talk more about the pain than they do the "Pain Reliever."

I have endured much pain in my life, some stuff I opened the door to willingly and other things were forced on me, but, if God allowed it to come it was necessary for my growth. I will not pretend that I went through all my painful seasons willingly.

There were many seasons I went through kicking and screaming because I did not understand the process at the time. I blamed a lot of my pain on the devil and people. I did not realize that God would cause pain to produce purpose. Listen to this, Isaiah 66:9(NCV) says,

In the same way I will not cause pain without allowing something new to be born," says the Lord. 'If I cause you the pain, I will not stop you from giving birth to your new nation," says your God.

You all better hear this scripture! If God has caused or allowed the pain, something great will be birthed out of it. It was not fun, but it was worth it. I must be honest, it is hard at times for me to pretend like my family were not willing vessels to be used by the enemy, and eagerly played victim and made me out to be the villain on many occasions. It was rough and while I was going through it I did not feel God's love, because I did not understand the love of God during that time, however, as I came into relationship with God and He took me on a journey through my mind. I could see and feel that His love was there. I still have the scars to remind me of what I had to endure, but the scars no longer have any effect on me. The scars are a reminder of my war, but it also reminds me that I made it through the war. My scars no longer bleed because I have allowed God to be a Balm to my wounds. I wanted to hate my family for what they did to me, but the power of God's love overshadowed the hate I was feeling which in return caused me to love them. God's love will make you love despite what has been done to you. Also, because of who God has called me to be in His Kingdom, I cannot walk in hate and unforgiveness. I feel sorry for them, because they have not repented and developed a real relationship with God. How I know is because they have the same odious behavior patterns. If I allowed them to do so, they would try to control my life as an adult. Everything they did to me they are trying to do with my daughter just not to the extreme they did with me. They have lied and played us against one another, but I finally woke up. My daughter is still asleep, but the only thing I can do for her is pray that God removes the scales from her eyes.

Their influence is powerful over you if you do not understand who you are and have the power of God on your side. The enemy thought that by using the people that was supposed to love me, their actions would prove to be harmful and would destroy my relationship with Christ, but when I received Christ as my personal Lord and Savior for real it made me stronger. The pain I had to endure brought on my change. The enemy's plan was defeated. He *tried to sift me as wheat, but God had other plans. I have a greater love for my painful process, I needed to go through it. I believe that is how God got the oil out of my life even when I did not know I was called to do Kingdom work. My painful seasons helped me understand people and how evil spirits can be utilized through them. Again, we must remember that this is not a flesh and blood battle. I have been through a lot of pain throughout my life, but nothing has been as great as having my daughter stolen from me.*

Yes, I believe she was stolen, and I will always believe it. When they came to get my daughter, they had an agenda. This is what makes the whole situation so sinister. I was supposed to be that family member that everybody else in the family was going to have to help, but God shifted the tables. The funny thing is my family see the change in my life, but they do not want to receive it. I am their Joseph, but they are trying to keep me in the pit. They fail to see that they are the ones with a pit mentality. It is amazing how your family can watch you go through situations and overcome, but still have a tainted lens of you. I am convinced that people can have more than you but are jealous of you because of the hand of God on your life. The hand of God cannot be denied on an individual, no matter what they have or do not have.

Some people may not know how to accurately articulate what they see on you, but they will detect that it is something different about you. I chose to grow from the dirt that was meant for my burial. My pain said, "God has something great for you on the other side of this fight through it." I had to learn while going through the process of my painful season not to focus on the faces of the people. I had to be intentional about remaining focused on God, especially when the demons within the people around me was vying for my attention. The pain I was dealt caused me to run to God. My pain was so great it caused me to run to the One I was supposed to have run from, because the intent was to make me hate God. I did not only run to God, I trusted Him with my pain, and because I chose to trust Him, He has trusted me with His people. That is another reason why I could not walk in hate, God has gifted me too mightily to wallow in an emotion that He has given me authority over. I have too much to lose operating any other way, but love. Yes, our gifts come without repentance, but I have seen many who are gifted, but have no anointing. I will not give Satan and his demons that much power over my life. I refuse to be a slave to the enemy. God allows us to go through painful seasons for a reason. The pain I endured helped in developing my spiritual muscle. It also helped me gain the wisdom I would need for my destiny. I still do not have the relationship that I once desired to have with my dad and stepmom, but I love them; I just do not have a desire to be a part of their lives until they develop a real relationship with Christ. I have tried so many times throughout the years, but it is hard to have a relationship with stagnate individuals who still thrive off trying to make your life a living hell.

What most believers do not realize is, it is not the person you are dealing with, you are dealing with the demon within the person, so trying to have a relationship with a demon will only get you wounded. These people turned my daughter against me. We have tried to build our relationship, but I can still feel the sting of their manipulation operating through her. Like I said earlier, she knows that they are liars, but once they talk to her, they can convince her that I am the liar. I want a relationship with my daughter, but all other buffoonery will have to be curbed. I am at a point in my life where I desire peace, and anything that comes to disturb my peace will get terminated. I no longer have that longing to have my dad in my life like I did when my inner little girl was in operation. God delivered and healed me from the little girl within when I was forty years old. I can now recognize when the enemy is using people for his diabolical ploy. When I needed them the most, they showed themselves to be deceivers.

Matthew 26:23(NIV) reminds us of what Jesus said, Jesus replied,

"The one who has dipped his hand into the bowl with me will betray me."

I broke bread with my Judas several times without knowing it, but there were many times I did know; it is sad when it is a parent. Let me take my stepmom out of the equation, now she played a major role, however, I am holding my dad responsible for his behavior and my stepmom's as well. I am the splitting image of my dad, but not only that, I am my dad's only child so why be a willing vessel for so much pain? I will probably never get the truth from him, but despite all the adversity I have grown from what was set out to destroy me. What was supposed to have killed me gave me life. John 10:10(NIV) helps us to understand that,

"The thief comes only to steal and kill and destroy; I have come that they may have life and have it to the full."

I am enjoying my life to the fullest.

Chapter 6

My Pain, My Salvation

It took having salvation and a real relationship with Christ to overcome what had come back from my past to sift me. I did not have a relationship with Christ when I left Alabama. I did receive Him as my personal Savior as a child, but when I became grown enough to understand I still had not developed a real relationship with Christ. I wanted to know about Jesus, so I would sit and listen to anyone that knew about Him. It was when I left Alabama and moved to Charlotte, I began to delve into a clearer understanding of who Christ was to me. Like I said earlier, a broken heart pushed me into the arms of Jesus, and sometimes it takes just that to get you where you need to be with our Savior.

I was a church goer. I had been going to church since I was a child. My grandmother sent me to church even when she did not go. I would walk to church even though she had a car, I did not mind because I could see and talk to all my friends. It was in me to go to church. I just did not have a real relationship with the Lord, but God knows how to lure us into the right situations to have to call on Him. God had been tugging at me, but I kept ignoring Him. When I moved to

Charlotte, I started hanging out with females that no matter what they did on Saturday they were pretty much getting up to go to church on Sunday. I did not see it then but that was God setting me up. After a few years I became a member of a church that one of the females I was hanging out with attended. I loved the way the Pastor ministered! There was also a woman that would get up to speak, she was a little woman with a bold gigantic voice, and I would be glued to her every word. I was still doing a lot of worldly things, but I knew that I wanted to do what I saw this amazing woman doing. I would tell people that I wanted to, one day, be a great speaker for God. I had no clue at the time what I was talking about. I just knew that I wanted to one day, do something for God. I eventually became an usher at the church. I was excited, but shortly after I became pregnant. I decided to stop ushering (I did not think it looked good ushering while pregnant out of wedlock.) While I was pregnant, I started to study my bible to gain a better understanding of who Jesus was. I mean, he took the feelings I had away for my two older boys dad, so I knew He was powerful. Other guys tried to do it, but they all failed. I cried out to Jesus and asked Him to remove the feelings, and a few days later they were gone, and I have not looked that way since. So, I had to find out who this Jesus was for real. After having my baby, I left the church that I attended and joined another church that was bigger. It was a little intimidating at first, but I felt led to join.

I was a single mom of three young boys and felt like an outcast at first, but I continued to go. One of the things that kept me going back was the way the Pastor preached. I had never heard anyone preach like he did in my life. He would preach all your business without personally knowing your business, so I knew he was different. I could not articulate it with words at the time, but I knew he was like no other preacher I had ever heard. Through his words came conviction; the kind of conviction that made you want to change and live right for God. I love my former Bishop for what he imparted in me, and I thank God for him. He had a God-given sound that I needed at the time and it kept my attention. I went on to receive my license to minister at this church. There were many other great leaders as well as members that helped encourage me and I am truly grateful. God took a single mom of three boys and raised her up to preach in the presence of many. By the time I got ready to preach my initial sermon I was married with another son. However, I was raised up before the people of God for some years as a single mother with three boys; that is what many of them referred to me as, the woman with the three boys. This proved to me that God could do whatever He wanted to do with whoever He wanted to do it through no matter their situation. God will take who people deem to be lesser than and put them at the head of the table. You just got to have a made-up mind to follow Him. The Word of God in Psalm 62:1(NIV) says:

"Truly my soul finds rest in God; my salvation comes from him."

My salvation came from the Lord. I am so glad that He loved me enough not to let me go even when I sinned against Him. God is a faithful God even when we are a faithless people. I received God s salvation, but it did not stop there, my salvation has turned into a wonderful relationship with my Father. I can rest knowing that God loves and cares for me.

Chapter 7
My Pain, My Gift

I had to go through great pain for the gifts God has entrusted me with.   Satan will come after you at birth when you are gifted. It is no different from what happened to Jesus when He was born. Matthew 2:13(NIV) says,

"When they had gone, an angel of the Lord appeared to Joseph in a dream. 'Get up', he said, 'take the child and his mother and escape to Egypt. Stay there until I tell you, for

Herod is going to search for the child to kill him.'"

Satan may not know in its entirety who God is calling you to be, but he catches a glimpse and because of this glimpse the attack commence. He came for me at birth and the reason why I say that is because of how it all started. I was conceived out of a sinful act. However, the

sinful act could not snuff out the gifts. The word in Romans 11:29(KJB) lets us know,

"For the gifts and calling of God are without repentance."

We are gifted before we are conceived, and because of this Satan plots to destroy many of us at an earlier age. I went through Hell over gifts that I did not even know I possessed. It is like being shot at by assassins, but you did not know that you were carrying something that would one day be used against them, but they did. You are just living your life. Looking back over my life, I can see that the hand of God was upon me even in my sin. God did something that no one in my family did, He invested in me, and even when I did not understand my worth, He still protected His investment. I had to go through what I went through so that I would not take my gifts for granted. I had to go through the pain of being gifted because I had to understand the weight of my call. Some people want to boast about being gifted but shun the pain that comes with the gift. You will have to embrace the pain to operate effectively in the gift. I did not understand this even while *knowing I was gifted. I was so focused on the pain that I did not realize that it was designed to help build my spiritual muscle. Therefore, it is mandatory that we stay focused on God during our painful seasons. We are to learn from the pain that has come to assist in the working of our growth. The enemy attacked me greatly through my family, but it was never about me or them, it was about the gifts I carried.*

The enemy wanted to abort my gifts, and he tried to do it through the people that meant the most to me; when something is aborted, it stops the life of it from coming forth. The enemy knows that our gifts will bring life to dead situations. Therefore, we are targets, the plan is to cause us to abort our destiny whether it is intentionally or unintentionally. That is why it is imperative that we keep our eyes on God versus the pain. Pain is a tool in your spiritual development and is never intended to be your master.

Chapter 8
My Pain, My Anointing

I said earlier that believers want to be anointed, but many shun the pain of going through the process to be anointed. We must embrace pain if we want to walk in the fullness of the anointing of the Lord. Even our Savior had to endure pain. Isaiah 53:5 (KJB:)

"But he was wounded for our transgressions, he was bruised for our iniquities"

The anointed One had to endure pain to display His love for a people that He knew would not love Him the same. Many people are anointed to go through the crushing of being anointed. It is like a washcloth that is being wrung out - you twist it until all the excess water is out. That is kind of what it feels like God is doing with us. He wrings us until the oil is produced. You are not officially anointed until you go through the wringing process. The wringing process hurts, oh my God it hurts, but it is needed for your oil to be birthed forth. When we go through trials and *tribulations it is because we have been anointed to endure it. Trials and tribulations set the oil in motion and causes it to flow through. If it had not been for my trials, I would not be anointed to do what God has called me to do.*

Having to endure the pain of being anointed is mandatory. There is no getting around it. There are many leaders that minister publicly but they are not producing any oil. Allow me to say this: it is not that they did not go through the wringing process, but because they have switched partners the anointing on their lives have grown stale. I mean, why go through such a crushing to only one day end up dry? It is so easy for our oil to become contaminated we must be incredibly careful. The enemy will set us up to contaminate our oil. That is why it is imperative that we guard it. We must be mindful of our relationships, friendships, connections etc. Satan wants to distort your oil and he will send spiritual assassins to do it, and sometimes the assassin can be self. We can be our own assassin when it comes to our oil. We mishandle our oil when we do not understand that our oil is not given to us for us to say, "we're anointed." It is given to us from our Father for Kingdom business. The anointing many of us possess is not for show; it is to affect and infect the lives of others and set them on Holy Ghost fire. Many of us have played with our anointing as if it will not dry up. This is the very reason why so many are preaching, but there is no power. There is no power because there is no oil!!! I do not ever want to be gifted but dry, and this is the state of many believers. It is vital that we take the anointing seriously. We were not crushed by God to get crushed by the enemy. We were crushed by God in order to crush the enemy. GUARD YOUR OIL! God sent you through the wringer for a reason, so do not mishandle or misuse your oil. I thank God for the oil He bestowed upon me, it has kept me relevant. The oil will keep you relevant. Yes, ultimately God keeps us relevant, but the oil on our lives is a symbol of God's relevant purpose for our lives. Again, GUARD YOUR OIL!!!

Chapter 9:
My Pain, My Feelings and Emotions

It is so easy to get caught up in our feelings and emotions when going through our painful seasons. I personally allowed my feelings and emotions to master me in my seasons of pain. Our feelings and emotions can cause us to act out of character and go against the will of God. Satan can use our pain to fight against us, and that is why he uses our feelings and emotions as tools to assist in his fiendish plot. When going through seasons of pain we must give God our feelings and emotions. I am not saying that we will not be emotional during these seasons, but what we cannot do is allow it to drive us. Being in my feelings and emotions caused me to want to fight individuals even while saved. I was sanctified filled with the Holy Ghost but would fight you if need be. I did not understand spiritual warfare during my time of pain. I just lashed out when I was crossed. That is what I was accustomed to doing, fighting back. God had to teach me how to fight spiritually versus naturally.

When enduring seasons of pain, we must push pass feelings and emotionalism and press into the purpose behind our pain. I am intentionally saying feelings and emotions repeatedly, because in this chapter I want you to get this way down in your spirit. It is crucial that we understand how dangerous our feelings and emotions can be. When we operate out of our feelings and emotions it can hinder what God is trying to root out of us. Painful seasons come to bring healing and deliverance, and if we do not recognize how our pain can be of help, we will remain climbing or going around the same mountain instead of speaking to it.

Mark 11:23-24 (NKJV) reminds us:

23. For assuredly, I say to you, whoever says to this mountain, 'Be removed and be cast into the sea', and does not doubt in his heart, but believes that those things he says will be done, he will have whatever he says. 24. Therefore I say to you, whatever things you

ask when you pray, believe that you receive them, and you will have them.

Feelings and emotions will keep us so engulfed that we forget we can speak to our mountain even while going through painful seasons. Pain produces a different kind of prayer life. However, as we pray, we must not doubt. When we doubt and do not believe it will place a bridle over our tongue and keep us from speaking to the mountain. Not only does it place a bridle over our tongue it binds the hands of God. Our feelings and emotions can stifle our growth if we do not place them in the hands of God. I fought in the natural due to being consumed by my feelings and emotions. I cussed some people out because I was allowing my feelings and emotions to be my master during a season, I should have embraced my pain and allowed God to do His work. However, it took a minute, but I finally spoke to the mountain embraced my pain and the work of God flowed forth. Get out of your feelings and emotions and watch God do a work that will shift you to a place of power. A power that will befuddle the people that have their eyes on you

Chapter 10

My Pain, My God

If it were not for God's covering, I would probably be dead or full of so much hate I would become a walking corpse. One of God's attributes is stickability. God stuck with me despite me. There was nothing that I could have done to make God detach Himself from me. He proved to me time after time and fall after fall that He was permanently in my life, and nothing or anyone could ever come between the love He had for me. Going through my painful seasons made the bond we have even stronger. There were times I threatened to walk away because my pain was so great. God took me through a journey in my mind, and there was a person within me, I really did not like.

Also, I had to revisit some past hurts that I had suppressed. I was the kind of person who had different compartments within me, and I would frequently pull out the hurt others had caused which would put me in a place mentally that would have me feeling some kind of way about the people I professed to forgive. Some years back I was sitting in my living room rehearsing in my mind some things people had done to me. God spoke to me and said,

"Have you really forgiven them?"

God had to show me that when we make the choice to forgive, we do not rehearse what has happened to us over and over in our mind, nor do we talk about it in a negative manner. When I went through my painful seasons it caused me to look at me and not the others around me. Going through seasons of pain is for your benefit; that is why it will behoove us not to go through these seasons wanting to blame others. During this time God is wanting to break us free from what people did to us and bring us into a full understanding of why He allowed us to endure what we went through. When we yield to our painful seasons God can do a stripping within our mind, heart and spirit. It will help us see things differently. It also helps us handle people differently. It is God's desire that we see the pain that we had to endure through new lenses. This causes us to operate in love despite the way people have handled us. When going through painful seasons we must remember that God is our strong tower. Proverbs 18:10 (NKJV) reminds us of this,

"The name of the Lord is a strong tower; The righteous run to it and are safe."

During seasons of pain we must understand that God is our dwelling place. We must run to Him versus running from Him. God loves each one of us. He allowed us to go through painful seasons so that He could display His love, and while we were in the midst of what was supposed to have killed us He caused us to gain wisdom, knowledge, understanding and a revelation that we would have never learned just by going to church. It was something we had to go through in order to gain a clearer understanding of our loving Father.

Chapter 11
My Pain,
My Conclusion

My conclusion of part one of this book is to remind you of how urgent it is to stay focused on God while going through painful seasons. Painful seasons will come, but they come to prepare us for our purpose. Painful seasons come to grow and groom us during our pain. Painful seasons come to teach us how to focus on God and not the people who assisted in our pain. We must stay in the ring during our painful seasons and not throw in the towel. Throwing the towel in is a sign of fleshly weakness. Listen to this! Going through pain will cause you to become weak because it is sent to zap your strength, however, when our strength is zapped God replaces it with His strength. That is why we must keep our attention on God, because the enemy wants to delude our thinking and cause us to give up right at the cusp of our breakthrough.

During our painful seasons we will experience God on a level that will help us understand His attributes.

Many of us claim to know God but we fail to fully understand His attributes; that is why it is imperative that we allow God to do an inward work in us while going through our pain. The pain has not come to obliterate us, but instead, comes to bring us to a place in God that gives healing, deliverance, wholeness and restoration. It is up to us to receive our seasons of pain so that we can walk in the full glory of God. Going through pain helps us to be effective and equipped for the Kingdom work God is calling us to do. It is a mandatory necessity that we allow our pain to come in for a season or seasons to do its perfect work. Going through pain is God's perfect work for our lives believe it or not. I understand that it is hard to comprehend how going through pain can be seen as a good thing however, when we trust God and take Him at His word, we will reap the benefits of yielding to our painful seasons. You want to be anointed and powerful for real? Stop holding on to pride and embrace your pain. Allow pain to push you into your destiny.

12. Dear friends, do not be surprised at the fiery ordeal that has come on you to test you, as though something strange were happening to you. 13. But rejoice inasmuch as you participate in the sufferings of Christ, so that you may be overjoyed when his glory is revealed.

1 Peter 4:12-13(NIV)

Amen!!!

Connect with the Author

Terra DeVon was born in Dadeville, Alabama on May 8th, 1973. She now resides in Kannapolis, NC. The forty-seven-year-old mother of four sons, one daughter, and three granddaughters, has a passion and heart for broken women, however, the calling that rests on her life is a corporate anointing that goes beyond ministering to just women but also men as well. At a young age her grandmother would send her to church many times walking alone, but Terra did not mind - she loved going to Sunday school, singing in the children's choir as well as seeing her friends. She accepted Christ at an early age not fully understanding the gift she had received.

When Terra became an adult, she would listen to anyone that had anything to say about God. She had a thirst for Godly knowledge and was trying to obtain an understanding that she did not have when she first accepted Jesus as her personal Lord and Savior. As she grew in her relationship with the Lord by reading, studying, praying, and joining a Bible based church that preached sound doctrine, it was then she recognized her call to ministry. Terra went through

Minister's in training where she received her license in 2013 by The Park Church in Charlotte, N.C. to function in ministry. Terra has operated in her gift of exaltation at conferences, revivals, retreats and day-to-day life. She not only operates in the gift of exaltation; she also operates in the office of a Prophetess. God has given her a unique sound for the Body of Christ. A sound that rattles the gates of hell and frustrates the devil and his imps. The message God has placed within Terra is for a time such as this. "When God Allows Pain to Be A Factor" is one of many books that will be birthed. This is the hour where God will use her voice to bring salvation, healing, deliverance and repentance to the Body.

'

www.ingramcontent.com/pod-product-compliance
Lightning Source LLC
Chambersburg PA
CBHW052157090426
42741CB00010B/2308